OUR BILL OF RIGHTS

NO UNREASONABLE SEARCHES AND SEIZURES

A LOOK AT THE THIRD AND FOURTH AMENDMENTS

RACHAEL MORLOCK

PowerKiDS press™

NEW YORK

Published in 2019 by The Rosen Publishing Group, Inc.
29 East 21st Street, New York, NY 10010

Editor: Sharon Gleason
Book Design: Rachel Rising

Photo Credits: Cover Yellow Dog Productions/The Image Bank/Getty Images; Cover, pp. 1, 3, 4, 5, 6, 7, 8, 10, 11, 12, 13, 14, 15, 16, 17, 18 ,19, 20, 21, 22, 24, 25, 26, 27, 28, 30, 31, 32 Mad Dog/Shutterstock.com; Cover, pp. 1, 3, 4, 5, 6, 7, 8, 10, 11, 12, 13, 14, 15, 16, 17, 18 ,19, 20, 21, 22, 24, 25, 26, 27, 28, 30, 31, 32 Flas100/Shutterstock.com; pp. 5, 13 MPI/Stringer/Getty Images; p. 6 (insert) Jack R Perry Photography/Shutterstock.com; p. 6 (background) Stone Master/Shutterstock.com; pp. 7, 11 Culture Club/Hulton Archive/Getty Images; pp. 8, 20 Forest Foxy/Shutterstock. com; p. 9 Stuart Monk/Shutterstock.com; p. 15 Buyenlarge/Archive Photos/Getty Images; p. 17 (insert) Orhan Cam/ Shutterstock.com; p. 17 https://commons.wikimedia.org/wiki/File:Supreme_Court_of_the_United_States_-_Roberts_ Court_2017.jpg; p. 18 larry1235/Shutterstock.com; p. 19 Digital Vision/Photodisc/Getty Images; p. 21 Stock Montage/ Archive Photos/Getty Images; p. 23 Monika Gruszewicz/Shutterstock.com; p. 25 Photo Researchers/Science Source/ Getty Images; p. 27 Rena Schild/Shutterstock.com; p. 29 Monkey Business Images/Shutterstock.com; p. 30 Bloomicon/Shutterstock.com.

Library of Congress Cataloging-in-Publication Data

Names: Morlock, Rachael, author.
Title: No unreasonable searches and seizures : a look at the third and fourth
    amendments / Rachael Morlock.
Description: New York : PowerKids Press, 2019. | Series: Our Bill of Rights |
    Includes index.
Identifiers: LCCN 2018019272| ISBN 9781538342985 (library bound) | ISBN
    9781538342961 (pbk.) | ISBN 9781538342978 (6 pack)
Subjects: LCSH: Searches and seizures--United States--Juvenile literature. |
    Privacy, Right of--United States--Juvenile literature. | United States.
    Constitution. 3rd Amendment--Juvenile literature. | United States.
    Constitution. 4th Amendment--Juvenile literature.
Classification: LCC KF9630 .M67 2019 | DDC 345.73/0522--dc23
LC record available at https://lccn.loc.gov/2018019272

Manufactured in the United States of America

CPSIA Compliance Information: Batch #CWPK19 For further information contact Rosen Publishing, New York, New York at 1-800-237-9932.

CONTENTS

THE BILL OF RIGHTS

After the Revolutionary War, Americans worked to shape an independent nation. Their first constitution, the Articles of Confederation, joined the states under a weak central government. In 1787, the Constitutional Convention met to consider changes to the federal government's powers. Members ended up creating an entirely new constitution.

Strengthening the government while also protecting the rights of citizens was a challenge. Some believed the U.S. Constitution was incomplete unless it clearly spelled out those rights. Others viewed a Bill of Rights as unnecessary.

This **debate** grew when the states considered the Constitution. A number of the states that **ratified** the Constitution also sent suggestions for a Bill of Rights. James Madison, a delegate from Virginia, ranked and edited their proposals. By popular demand, the Third and Fourth Amendments, or changes, were among the 10 that became the Bill of Rights.

In 1787, 39 delegates signed the U.S. Constitution in Philadelphia, Pennsylvania. George Mason, an anti-Federalist who argued for a Bill of Rights, was one of three delegates who refused to sign.

KNOW YOUR RIGHTS!

The Federalists preferred a strong central government and criticized the call for a Bill of Rights. In their view, the Constitution's division of power already guarded against tyranny and protected rights.

YOUR HOUSE IS YOUR CASTLE

All the amendments in the Bill of Rights were designed to limit the government's power. Having fought a war for freedom, the Constitution's framers were anxious to build a fair government. They hoped to ensure liberty and **amplify** the voice of the people.

BILL OF RIGHTS

In 1628, the English judge Sir Edward Coke famously claimed that "a man's house is his castle." This meant that all dwellings were important to their owners and deserved legal protections.

Together, the Third and Fourth Amendments protect citizens' rights to property and privacy. Although the British had denied colonial Americans these rights, English law included provisions for both. A popular idea in England was that the home, regardless of size or quality, was a sacred space. This inspired laws that protected private homes from both criminals and government officials. As Madison created the Bill of Rights, he looked to English and American **precedents** that guarded the privacy and property of citizens.

THE THIRD AMENDMENT

The Third Amendment states "No Soldier shall, in time of peace be quartered in any house, without the consent of the Owner, nor in time of war, but in a manner to be prescribed by law." Quartering means providing lodging for soldiers. By "house," the amendment refers to inns, hotels, homes, barns, and other privately owned buildings. Overall, the amendment protects private property from use by the military.

The amendment contains several important parts. First, it bans quartering troops on private property during peacetime without permission from the owner. The amendment does not fully ban quartering during war but limits it. In wartime, the amendment allows quartering only if Congress passes clear laws regulating it.

The Third Amendment limits the ways members of the military can use the private property of citizens.

UNJUST ACTS

The Constitution's framers worked to form a government that would **guarantee** the rights of the people. The Bill of Rights aimed to prevent the tyranny and unfair treatment Americans had experienced under British rule.

Unpopular and unjust British policies led directly to the Third Amendment. The Quartering Act of 1765 made colonists financially responsible for the food, housing, and transportation of British soldiers in peacetime. In 1774, the British lawmaking body passed a new version of the Quartering Act. It gave British soldiers the right to use colonists' barns, inns, and empty houses.

Many Americans had been forced to house soldiers on their property. The Founding Fathers created the Third Amendment in response. It required soldiers to respect the property of American citizens.

KNOW YOUR RIGHTS!

The Quartering Act of 1774 was passed along with other unfair taxes on Americans. The Intolerable Acts, as they were called by colonists, sparked greater resistance to the British government.

STANDING ARMIES

Quartering bans were partly related to popular opinions about standing armies. American colonists viewed standing, or permanent and professional, armies as a dangerous threat to freedom. They objected to the costs of maintaining an army during peacetime. They also worried about unchecked military power, especially after the Boston Massacre, when British soldiers fired on citizens. Instead, most Americans preferred to rely on local **militias** in times of war.

When British troops sailed into Boston in 1768, the Quartering Act forced colonists to pay for the soldiers' needs. Pressure built up between soldiers and colonists, resulting in the Boston Massacre of 1770.

AN AMERICAN VALUE

Rules against quartering existed long before the Bill of Rights. Laws forbidding quartering are found in an English charter from 1131. The idea was also included in the English Bill of Rights of 1689. However, quartering repeatedly took place in America as a way to support the British armies.

As a result, Americans valued quartering controls. As early as 1683, New York attempted to protect its residents from quartering in its Charter of Liberties and Privileges. After the Revolution, several state constitutions included laws against quartering.

While the states were ratifying the U.S. Constitution, Patrick Henry notably insisted it should include a quartering **prohibition**. He said that quartering was a major cause of the American Revolution. Along with Henry's state, Virginia, four other states suggested adding quartering rules to the Constitution.

British troops occupied New York City during the Revolutionary War, quartering in camps and private buildings. While ratifying the Constitution, more states recommended quartering amendments than free speech provisions.

KNOW YOUR RIGHTS!

The Declaration of Independence lists quartering as a reason for the American Revolution. It accuses King George III of "quartering large bodies of armed troops among us."

VIOLATIONS

Today, many people think the Third Amendment is unnecessary or outdated. The United States government has unlawfully quartered soldiers in its history. There have been three important periods of Third Amendment **violations**.

During the War of 1812, the Civil War, and World War II, American soldiers were quartered on private property. According to the Third Amendment, wartime quartering is allowed if it is "prescribed by law." However, Congress didn't pass laws that allowed military quartering in these cases.

In 1942, during World War II, residents of the Aleutian Islands of Alaska were removed from their homes and sent to **internment camps**. The U.S. military occupied and destroyed their property while observing enemy forces. More than 40 years later, the U.S. government offered a payment to the survivors.

HURRICANE KATRINA

There is evidence of Third Amendment violations in the confusion following Hurricane Katrina. After the hurricane in 2005, the National Guard was sent to Louisiana and Mississippi to help. There were few available housing options for relief workers. In some cases, the National Guard seized and occupied private property. This situation raises important questions about Third Amendment protections in the event of natural or national disasters, or tragedies.

Congress passed laws during the Civil War that allowed quartering in Confederate states. However, there were no laws regarding the private property in loyal states that Union troops used for hospitals and shelters.

INTERPRETING THE THIRD AMENDMENT

What happens when an amendment is violated? The Supreme Court, the highest court in the United States, is responsible for protecting the Constitution by ruling on important cases. It guards the rights of the people and determines if laws are constitutional. The Supreme Court also **interprets** the Constitution within the framework of modern life.

In the more than 200 years since the Bill of Rights was ratified, no Supreme Court case has been specifically concerned with quartering troops. However, the Third Amendment has been used to interpret other individual rights. If the amendment was meant to prevent military **intrusions** into private homes, then what other intrusions are unconstitutional? The Third Amendment has been called on, together with the Fourth Amendment, to point to a constitutional right to privacy.

KNOW YOUR RIGHTS!

In the Supreme Court case *Griswold v. Connecticut* (1965), the court referred to the Third and Fourth Amendments, as well as others. The decision established the idea that the Constitution protects "zones of privacy" in citizens' lives.

ENGBLOM V. CAREY

One court case has dealt specifically with the Third Amendment. In 1982, a U.S. court of appeals heard *Engblom v. Carey*. The court found that New York State violated the Third Amendment during a prison workers' strike. The workers, who lived on the prison grounds, were barred from their residences. They were replaced in their jobs and homes by National Guard members. Even though the court determined that this was unconstitutional, the state still won the case.

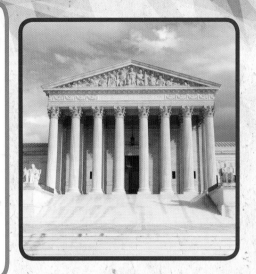

The Supreme Court is made up of nine justices. They ensure that the Constitution is a "living document," which means it is an official written record that can adapt to the changing needs of the country.

THE FOURTH AMENDMENT

The Fourth Amendment joins the Third Amendment in protecting privacy: "The right of the people to be secure in their persons, houses, papers, and effects, against unreasonable searches and seizures, shall not be violated, and no Warrants shall issue, but upon probable cause, supported by Oath or affirmation, and particularly describing the place to be searched, and the persons or things to be seized."

If there is enough evidence that someone may have committed a crime, a judge will sign a search warrant. Then, police officers can search a citizen's home.

The amendment guarantees that a citizen's home, belongings, and self are private and protected from unreasonable government searches and seizures. Next, it outlines rules government officials must follow before violating that privacy. There must be clear, provable reasons for searching or taking a citizen's property. With the warrants mentioned, searches and seizures of people and their private property may be lawful.

"THE RIGHT TO BE LET ALONE"

The Fourth Amendment limits government contact with Americans' private lives. As Supreme Court Justice Louis Brandeis noted in a 1927 case (and the court later agreed), the Fourth Amendment represents "the right to be let alone." Judges and police are only supposed to allow searches and seizures if there are clear signs that a law has been broken.

Like the Third Amendment, the Fourth Amendment was influenced by events before the American Revolution. Some colonists smuggled goods in order to avoid increasingly heavy British taxes. In response, British officials used "writs of assistance" to search any American or their property for untaxed items. Writs of assistance, or court orders, and general, or open-ended, warrants authorized the British to search homes and arrest colonists. As a result, the Founding Fathers created the Fourth Amendment, which requires that all warrants be specific and reasonable.

Colonial lawyer James Otis passionately opposed writs of assistance, stating that Americans possessed the same natural and legal right to privacy as people in Great Britain.

JAMES OTIS

In 1761, James Otis resigned from his British post in order to protest writs of assistance. Otis believed writs were unlawful and fought against them in court on behalf of Boston merchants. Although he lost the case, his stirring arguments alerted Americans to the dangers of **arbitrary** British power and inspired resistance. John Adams gave Otis credit for planting the seeds of American independence.

21

REASONABLE AND UNREASONABLE

Despite the use of general warrants in America, English law did restrict unreasonable searches and seizures. Sir Edward Coke opposed arbitrary searches and argued for protection of private homes in 1604. In important cases in 1763 and 1765, judges ruled that general warrants in England were illegal.

This British tradition, along with their colonial experiences, encouraged Americans to seek legal protection from random, or unplanned, searches and warrants. After the Revolution, several states outlawed general warrants in their constitutions, and some of them recommended warrant protections in the Bill of Rights.

The wording of the Fourth Amendment only prohibits unreasonable searches and seizures. That means that some violations of privacy are legal. In order for a search to be reasonable and legal, there must be clear evidence that a crime may have been committed.

KNOW YOUR RIGHTS!

If there is "probable cause" for a search or seizure, it means that there is good reason to believe that a specific person has broken a specific law.

The Fourth Amendment is meant to prevent citizens from being arrested unreasonably.

THE WARRANT CLAUSE

The second part of the Fourth Amendment is the warrant clause. It creates a framework for obtaining warrants. These warrants must include exact information about who and what will be searched or seized. Judges must approve warrants.

However, legal cases have established many exceptions to the warrant clause. Several Supreme Court cases have included rulings on general situations that permit searches and seizures without probable cause or warrants. These include "stop-and-frisk" police practices, airport security, drug testing, and student searches.

A second category of exceptions includes cases where probable cause is present, but a warrant isn't required. For example, police who witness a crime can make arrests without a warrant. These exceptions are meant to improve public safety.

KNOW YOUR RIGHTS!

The exclusionary rule says that evidence found as the result of an unlawful search cannot be used in a court case. The rule aims to prevent law enforcement officials from performing illegal searches.

AIRPORT SECURITY

When the Founding Fathers wrote the Fourth Amendment, the focus was on investigating crimes. Today, police and security officers also work to prevent crimes. That means that people and their property can sometimes be searched even if they're not suspected of a crime. An example of this is airport security. In an effort to improve safety and prevent crime, all passengers are screened, or checked, without probable cause.

Many police searches can be made without a warrant if there is probable cause. The courts have ruled that automobile searches don't require warrants.

THE COST OF SAFETY

In modern society, privacy and crime involve many factors that the Constitution's framers never saw coming. The Fourth Amendment must now be interpreted in respect to the Internet, electronic **surveillance**, and **terrorism**. As a result, security is changing. Citizens and courts must balance personal privacy with public safety.

In the last century, surveillance techniques included wiretapping, or listening to phone calls, and bugging, or using small microphones to record conversations. Today, the government can collect private information without warrants by studying Internet data and communication patterns. Drones are also potential surveillance tools.

Since September 11, 2001, pressure on the Fourth Amendment has increased. Legislation such as the USA PATRIOT Act and the USA Freedom Act compromises personal privacy to increase national security. Privacy may be the cost of safety.

THE USA PATRIOT ACT

The USA PATRIOT Act was signed on October 26, 2001. The terrorist attack on September 11 that year influenced legislators to pass the act. It gave law enforcement officers more powers to detect terrorist activities by allowing surveillance without warrants. Critics of the PATRIOT Act question if the benefits of surveillance outweigh the loss of privacy.

In 2013, Edward Snowden released classified information about the National Security Agency (NSA). Snowden believed the NSA violated the Fourth Amendment by tracking the phone and Internet activity of ordinary citizens.

SEARCHES AND SEIZURES AT SCHOOL

Several important Supreme Court cases have examined student rights and exceptions to the Fourth Amendment. In the 1985 case *New Jersey v. T. L. O.*, the Supreme Court ruled that schools don't need warrants to search student belongings. Schools are responsible for supervising students and providing a safe environment. As a result, school officials can legally search students' backpacks, lockers, and property.

In the 1995 case of *Vernonia School District v. Acton*, the Supreme Court decided that schools can legally test students on athletic teams for drug use. Another case in 2002 approved drug testing for students participating in other school activities. These decisions emphasize that, in many cases, a student's right to privacy is subject to school rules and lies outside the Fourth Amendment's protections.

Like the government, schools must strike a balance between respecting students' rights and keeping safety and order.

AMERICAN IDEALS

The Third and Fourth Amendments are critical to the Bill of Rights. They stress the importance of privacy and protect citizens' homes and lives from unnecessary invasions. They set boundaries and control the government and military in private life. America is constantly changing, but the respect for privacy found in the Third and Fourth Amendments will always be necessary.

As a whole, the Bill of Rights limits government power. The Constitution's framers wanted the government to serve rather than rule the people. By spelling out important freedoms, the Bill of Rights gives citizens the power to shape the government, society, and their own lives. Americans can rely on the Constitution and amendments to protect and guide them.

GLOSSARY

amplify: To make greater or stronger.

arbitrary: Done without thought to fairness or right.

debate: A discussion or argument between two teams or sides.

guarantee: To promise.

internment camp: A place where people are confined, especially during a war.

interpret: To explain or judge the meaning of an idea or statement.

intrusion: An unwelcome entry by force.

militia: A group of citizens with some military training called to duty in an emergency.

precedent: Something that may serve as an example or rule to be followed in the future.

prohibition: An order that stops something from being done.

ratify: To give legal or official approval.

surveillance: Close observation, especially of a suspected criminal or spy.

terrorism: The use of terror or violence as a means of achieving a goal.

violation: An instance of failing to respect someone's rights.

INDEX

WEBSITES

Due to the changing nature of Internet links, PowerKids Press has developed an online list of websites related to the subject of this book. This site is updated regularly. Please use this link to access the list: www.powerkidslinks.com/obor/thirdfourth